SEATTLE PUBLIC LIBRARY

1/10
- 1/2014-12/14
11/2015-1/16
- 7/2017-11/17

WE: LIBRARY

JUN 1 1 2001

WEST SEATTLE LIBRARY

JUN 1 1 2001

NO LONGER PROPERTY OF
SEATTLE PUBLIC LIBRARY

D1120120

Native Americans

Northwest Coast Indians

Mir Tamim Ansary

Heinemann Library
Des Plaines, Illinois

© 2000 Reed Educational & Professional Publishing
Published by Heinemann Library,
an imprint of Reed Educational & Professional Publishing,
1350 East Touhy Avenue, Suite 240 West
Des Plaines, IL 60018
Customer Service: 888-454-2279

All rights reserved. No part of this publication may be
reproduced or transmitted in any form or by any means,
electronic or mechanical, including photocopying, recording,
taping, or any information storage and retrieval system,
without permission in writing from the publisher.

Designed by Depke Design

Printed in Hong Kong

04 03 02 01 00
10 9 8 7 6 5 4 3 2

Library of Congress Cataloging-in-Publication Data
Ansary, Mir Tamim
        Northwest Coast Indians / Mir Tamim Ansary.
            p. cm. – (Native Americans)
        Includes bibliographical references (p.   ) and index.
        Summary: Introduces the history, dwellings, artwork, religious
    beliefs, clothing, food, and other elements of life of the Native
    American tribes of the Pacific Northwest.
        ISBN 1-57572-921-0 (library binding)
        1. Indians of North America—Northwest Coast of North America
    Juvenile literature. [1. Indians of North America—Northwest Coast
    of North America.] I. Title. II. Series: Ansary, Mir Tamim.
        Native Americans.
    E78.N78A57 1999
    979.5'00497—dc21   99-13517
                                                  CIP

Acknowledgments
The publisher would like to thank the following for permission to reproduce photographs:
Cover: Corbis-Bettmann
Donna Ikenberry/Animals Animals, p. 4; National Geographic/Richard Schlecht, p. 7; The
Granger Collection, pp. 8, 19, 20, 21, 30 top; Corbis-Bettmann, pp. 9, 10, 11, 14, 16, 17, 18, 23;
David Neel, pp. 12, 22, 29, 30 bottom; Lawrence Migdale, pp. 13, 26; Bridgeman Art Library
International Ltd., p. 15; Erich Lessing/Art Resource, p. 24; Stock Montage, Inc., p. 25; Shane
Moore/Animals Animals, p. 27; John De Visser/Masterfile, p. 28.

Every effort has been made to contact copyright holders of any material reproduced in this
book. Any omissions will be rectified in subsequent printings if notice is given to the publisher.

Our special thanks to Lana Grant, Native American MLS, for her help
in the preparation of this book.

Note to the Reader Some words are shown in bold, **like this.** You can find
out what they mean by looking in the glossary.

Contents

Between Mountains and Sea

North of California is an area called the Pacific Northwest. It stretches between the Pacific Ocean and the Cascade Mountains. The peaks of these mountain are always capped with snow. Their **slopes** come down almost to the sea. Little bays dot the rocky coast.

This is a land of **mist** and rain. Few days are really hot or really cold. Most days, however, are wet. Trees grow tall, and forests are **lush** with moss. From almost everywhere here, you can hear the sound of rushing water.

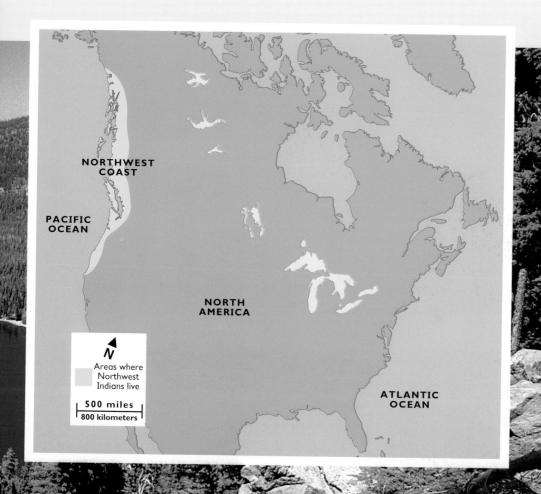

NORTHWEST
COAST

PACIFIC
OCEAN

NORTH
AMERICA

N

Areas where
Northwest
Indians live

500 miles
800 kilometers

ATLANTIC
OCEAN

The Earliest People

People started moving to this land at least 8,000 years ago. Some came by sea from the north. Some came by land from the south. Some came over the mountains. They settled along the coast and formed many tribes. These people were the Haida, Chinook, Tlinget, Makah, and many others.

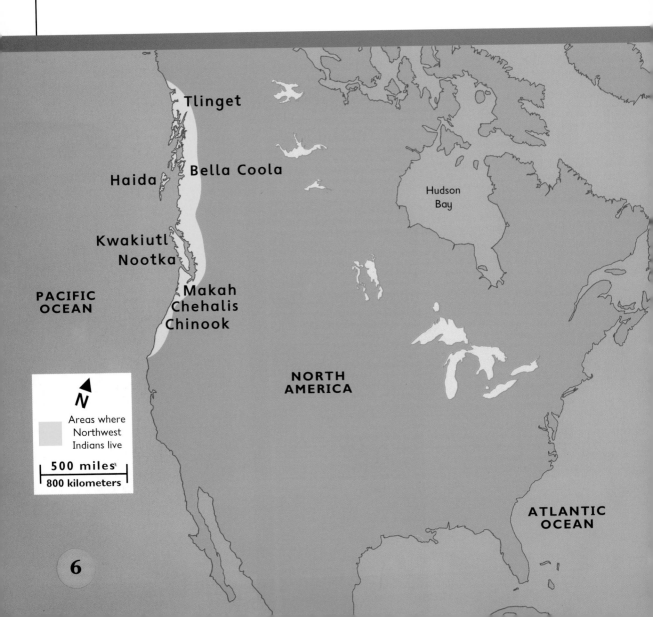

Tlinget

Haida

Bella Coola

Hudson Bay

Kwakiutl
Nootka

PACIFIC
OCEAN

Makah
Chehalis
Chinook

N

Areas where
Northwest
Indians live

500 miles
800 kilometers

NORTH
AMERICA

ATLANTIC
OCEAN

Ozette is a Makah village near present-day Seattle. About 400 years ago, a mud slide buried parts of this village. The mud **preserved** the houses. Now they have been dug up again. From these houses, we can see how the people of the Pacific Northwest lived before they met Europeans.

Ozette may have looked something like this 400 years ago.

Land of Plenty

Native Americans of the Northwest Coast didn't farm—they didn't have to. The forests were full of nuts, berries, and **game**. The rivers were full of salmon and other fish. One of these was the candlefish. It was so rich in oil, people could dry it and light it like a candle.

These Pacific Northwest Indians are using nets to catch whitefish in the Columbia River.

This Nootka hunter is wearing a sealskin coat and is holding a harpoon.

People got food from the ocean as well. They caught big fish such as halibut. They hunted walruses and seals. They chased whales in huge dugout canoes carved from single logs. They killed these sea mammals with **harpoons.**

Homes of Wood

Since trees were plentiful, people built their houses out of wood. They cut trees into poles and planks with stone axes. They used wooden pegs to hold their houses together. One house might be as big as 80 feet (24 meters) long and 50 feet (15 meters) wide.

The door on a Northwest Coast house like this one always faced the ocean or beach.

Notice the sleeping stalls along the side walls. Each stall was for a different family.

Each huge house had just one room. However, the floor of this room had several levels. Along the walls were sleeping **stalls**. In the middle was a fire pit. A hole in the roof let out smoke. All the people in a house belonged to the same **clan**. This means that they shared **ancestors**.

Rainy Day Clothing

The Indians of the Pacific Northwest even made clothing out of trees. They didn't need much to stay warm, but they did need to stay dry. So they wove cone-shaped hats out of cedar bark. These hats worked like umbrellas. For extra protection, they often smeared themselves with bear grease.

Besides hats, people also made capes of bark to help keep dry in the Pacific Northwest.

This man and boy are wearing blankets woven on a half loom.

Tree bark was used to make cloth, too. The cloth was woven out of spruce bark and dog fur. The Tlinget were famous for their lovely "button blankets," which were decorated with sea shells. Blankets were used like money. They were traded for other useful items.

Trade and War

All the Northwest Indian tribes traded with each other. The greatest traders were the Chinook. They carried blankets, oil, and other **goods** up and down the rivers and coast. They traveled in big, beautiful canoes. Words from many languages mixed into Chinook. And most people spoke a little Chinook.

Canoes like this one were made from a single log hollowed out with fire.

Wooden armor like this protected a warrior's chest.

The Northwest Indians got goods through war as well as trade. They went into battle wearing armor made of wooden **slats.** They fought with wooden clubs. Often they captured slaves. The slaves were not made to do much work, however. They were kept as a way to show off the owner's wealth.

Giving Away Wealth

All over the Pacific Northwest, people gathered wealth just to give it away. People could rise in **rank** by giving **goods** away. A chief gave goods away at a special feast called a potlatch. The more he gave, the more important he became. Later his guests held a potlatch to keep up.

The host of this potlatch will give away blankets and other wealth as the feast goes on.

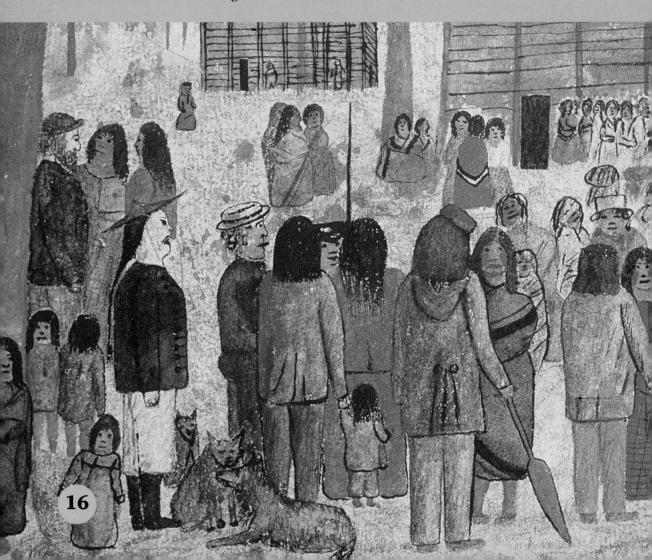

A Kwakiutl potlatch sometimes turned into a contest. Two rich chiefs might show off by wasting wealth, not just giving it away. They would burn blankets and break fancy plates called "coppers." The man who wasted less lost the contest. He sometimes had to leave his village in shame.

The woman in the fancy robe is holding a copper, a valuable plate.

Totems and Totem Poles

Indians of the Northwest Coast felt a great connection to animals. Every **clan** had its own totem or animal **spirit.** People painted pictures of their totems everywhere, even on their faces. Two strangers who had the same totem felt that they were **related.** This sense of connection to animals is still alive.

Totems, like this one, were like the family crests that European knights wore on their shields.

Totem poles were made only in the Pacific Northwest.

Many houses had totem poles outside. You can still see these sculptures in the Pacific Northwest. A totem pole is like a billboard. It shows what clan lives in a house. It shows scenes from clan history, too. A totem pole was a clan's way of boasting about its greatness.

Animal Tales

Animals showed up in many stories too. There was the raven, for example—a clever **trickster.** Sometimes the raven was too clever for its own good. Yet the raven was also respected, and remains respected today. It is seen as the **spirit** who created the world.

These ravens are painted on a wooden room divider.

Native Americans of the Pacific Northwest told tales about a thunderbird, which was something like a dragon. The thunderbird was said to live high in the mountains. It snatched killer whales out of the ocean and ate them. Storytellers still say the thunderbird creates storms.

A Kwakiutl artist made this thunderbird out of wood and abalone shells.

From Person to Animal

According to Indian religions of the Pacific Northwest, people and animals are alike inside. Kwakiutl beliefs say that long ago, animals could turn into people and people could turn into animals. Stories are told about these changes. In one story, a man kidnaps a princess. Then he becomes a bear and she becomes his wife.

Masks were used to tell stories about animals turning into people and people into animals.

The beak on this mask can open to show the actor's face inside.

Such stories are acted out in special religious dances. The dancers wear masks with moving parts. At first the mask shows an animal's face. At a special moment, the dancer pulls hidden strings. Suddenly the mask opens. Everyone sees the human face inside.

Europeans Arrive

Around 1800, white settlers started moving into the Pacific Northwest. Some came as **missionaries**. Some came to farm or log. At first, the Native Americans traded with them. They liked the Europeans' metal tools. With these tools, the Indians could carve even finer boxes, boats, and other items.

Teeth and shells were used to decorate this Haida storage box.

Astor's ship, the Tonquin, *was later wrecked by Nootka Indian warriors.*

But the settlers kept coming. They began to crowd the native people. Fights broke out. The Nootka got angry at a man named John Astor. He was getting rich from cutting down trees in their homeland. Nootka warriors sank his ship, the *Tonquin*. But Astor wouldn't go away.

Cities and Reservations

Slowly, the Native Americans were pushed off their lands. Some moved onto reservations—special areas set aside for Native Americans. Others settled in the growing cities. Today, about six out of every ten Pacific Northwest Indians live in cities. They work at the same jobs as non-Indians.

Today, Indians of the Pacific Northwest work in many different jobs.

Today in the Pacific Northwest, logging is a big business.

The reservation Indians try to keep some of the old ways alive. But many worry that logging is spoiling the rivers for fishing. They worry that the salmon will die out. Some tribes of the Pacific Northwest are fighting for their fishing rights. But they are fighting in **court.** Their warriors now are lawyers.

Old Ways, New Art

Many of the old ways are gone from the Pacific Northwest. Even the Chinook people no longer speak the Chinook language. But you can visit the K'san Historical Indian Village in Canada. The Gitk'san tribe runs this **living museum**. They make a living teaching people how their **ancestors** lived.

K'san Heritage Village is a favorite stop for tourists in British Columbia, Canada.

This is a mask made by David Neel, a famous modern-day Native American artist.

The Native American people of the Pacific Northwest are very much alive, however. They are still telling the old stories. They are making up new ones, too. Young artists from tribes such as the Kwakiutl are creating new art. This art is rooted in the past, but it is pointed toward the future. It is modern art.

Famous Northwest Coast Indians

Charles Edenshaw (Haida: 1839–1920). Edenshaw was chief of the Haida Eagle **clan.** He was also a great artist. He started carving at the age of fourteen. He made boxes, rattles, masks, totem poles, sculptures, and much more. Museums around the world now own and show his work.

Chief Seattle (Duwamish: 1786–1866) Chief Seattle worked for peace between his people and white settlers. The city of Seattle, Washington, was named after him. In 1855, he helped set up the first reservation for Washington tribes. He gave a great, sad speech at that time. His speech described the end of the Indian way of life.

David Neel (Kwakiutl: 1960–) Neel is a photographer and sculptor. His photographs show Native American life all across North America today. His work is seen in magazines, books, posters, and art shows across the country. His father, grandmother, great uncle, and great great grandfather were artists, too.

Glossary

ancestor someone who comes earlier in a family, especially someone before a grandparent

clan group of families that shares an ancestor

court place where a judge hears a case of law

game animals hunted to be eaten

goods items people use or want to own

harpoon spearlike weapon with big hooks at the end

living museum village, town, or group of buildings that recreates life in another time or place

lush rich with plant growth

missionary person who tries to get others to join his or her religion

mist fog so heavy it is almost rain

preserved saved from rotting or falling apart

rank higher or lower position in a group

related belonging to the same family

slat flat, narrow strip of wood

slope side of a mountain

stall booth or tiny room

spirit being that has life but cannot be seen

trickster one who plays clever tricks

More Books to Read

Beyer, Thomas R. *Indians of the Totem Pole.* Danbury, Conn.: Children's Press, 1991.

Brother Eagle, Sister Sky: A Message from Chief Seattle. New York: Dial Books for Young Readers, 1991

Hoyt-Goldsmith, Diane. *Potlatch: A Tsimshian Celebration.* New York: Holiday House, 1997.

Index